CALABASAS STREET

by
JOSÉ CRUZ GONZÁLEZ

Dramatic Publishing
Woodstock, Illinois • London, England • Melbourne, Australia

IMPORTANT BILLING AND CREDIT REQUIREMENTS

All producers of the Play *must* give credit to the Author(s) of the Play in all programs distributed in connection with performances of the Play and in all instances in which the title of the Play appears for purposes of advertising, publicizing or otherwise exploiting the Play and/or a production. The name of the Author(s) *must* also appear on a separate line, on which no other name appears, immediately following the title, and *must* appear in size of type not less than fifty percent the size of the title type. *On all programs this notice should appear:*

"Produced by special arrangement with
THE DRAMATIC PUBLISHING COMPANY of Woodstock, Illinois"

CALABASAS STREET was first presented by California State University, Los Angeles Theatre Arts & Dance Department on October 14-16, 21-23, 1994.

CAST

Michael Aparicio
Gaby Cerda
Susan Clay
Chrys Dulac
Maria Orlandi
Jennifer Uzan

PRODUCTION STAFF

Director . . . . José Cruz González
Set and Costume Design. . . . . G. Shizuko Herrera
Lighting Design . . . . Lonnie Alcaraz
Stage Manager . . . . Yuki Uehara

CALABASAS STREET was further developed at the HBO New Writers Project in September 1995.

CALABASAS STREET

A Play in One Act
For 2 Men and 4 Women

CHARACTERS

DOMINGO . . . . a college student,
transforms into an 8-year-old as he narrates

LA VIUDA MARTINEZ . . . an elderly Mexican-American
woman, a piñata maker. Her first name is Consuelo.

MIERCOLES . . . . Domingo's older sister, 11 years old

VIERNES . . . . Domingo's younger sister, 7 years old

DICIEMBRE. . . . . Domingo's mother, late 20s

KIKO. . . . . La Viuda Martinez's husband, a memory
(doubles as the School Bus Driver)

SETTING: Suggestive. Set pieces should be kept to a minimum. The piñata artwork should be a combination of papier-maché and sculpture work.

Running time: 45 minutes

For Maria Jesus González

CALABASAS STREET

AT RISE: *Music. Lights up on DOMINGO, a young man.*

DOMINGO. My name is Domingo Sanchez. And I grew up on Calabasas Street not far from here. My parents still live there. You might recognize their house. There's statues of the Virgen de Guadalupe, Pinocchio and the King, Elvis Presley.

(An OLD WOMAN dressed in black enters wheeling a small cart.)

You see that woman dressed in black? That's La Viuda Martinez. Everyone on Calabasas Street called her "la Loca"—the Crazy One. Why? Because she was always dressed in black, collected junk from garbage cans and liked smoking Cuban cigars. *(The OLD WOMAN spits loudly. She goes to a garbage can removing newspapers and cans, etc.)* Yuck! Everyone on Calabasas Street was afraid of her but they shouldn't have been. You know, sometimes the things we fear most are the things we least understand. I learned that one summer when I was still eight years old and Calabasas Street was the only world that mattered. La Viuda Martinez changed all that.

(MIERCOLES enters, followed by VIERNES.)

VIERNES. Mira, es la loca!

MIERCOLES. Be quiet! She might hear you! I heard she turns kids into rocks!

DOMINGO (*as a boy*). What's she doing?

VIERNES. Something crazy I bet.

MIERCOLES. Papí said to stay away from her. All she does is collect junk and takes it home.

VIERNES. Do you think she's a bruja?

MIERCOLES. Well, she's dressed in black, que no? All witches dress in black.

VIERNES. Look, she's even got a broom!

DOMINGO. She's coming this way!

MIERCOLES. Don't look in her eyes. She'll turn you into a rock! Run! Hide! (*They all cross themselves and exit except for DOMINGO. LA VIUDA MARTINEZ continues to collect junk.*)

DOMINGO (*as a young man*). La Viuda Martinez had lived on Calabasas Street for as long as I could remember. She was a viuda. Her husband had died long ago. She lived in an old house on Calabasas Street and it was the scariest looking house there was. Nobody ever wandered into her yard. It was like stepping into your worst nightmare. (*MARTINEZ spits loudly.*) Yuck! She had this disgusting habit of smoking cigars and spitting wherever she went. You could always tell where La Viuda Martinez had gone because she'd leave a trail of tobacco juice stains.

(*MARTINEZ spits and exits as MIERCOLES and VIERNES enter.*)

VIERNES. Look, Miercoles, la Loca's going into her house.

MIERCOLES. I heard lots of people went into that house and never came out, Viernes.

VIERNES. Really?

MIERCOLES. Some say she even killed her children.

DOMINGO (*as a boy*). Is she La Llorona?

MIERCOLES. Who knows, but you better watch out, Mocoso.

DOMINGO. Don't call me Mocoso!

MIERCOLES. Well, that's what Tio Agosto calls you. Don't be playing baseball out here by yourself because you might not come back home. La Loca might get you. I'd hate to tell Papí she got you.

VIERNES. He'd be real angry.

DOMINGO. I'll do what I please, Miercoles! I'll play baseball if I want to! La Loca doesn't own the block and neither do you!

MIERCOLES. Don't say I didn't warn you, little brother! Let's go, Viernes! (*MIERCOLES and VIERNES exit.*)

DOMINGO. There were six sisters in my family and I was the only boy. We were all named after each day of the week in Spanish. Can you imagine? There were the twins, Lunes and Martes, my older sister Miercoles, Jueves, the bookworm, Viernes, the tattletale and Sabado, in diapers. I was the born on a Sunday, so naturally I was named Domingo.

(*MIERCOLES enters sucking on a lollipop.*)

MERCOLES. La Llorona drowned all her children and now she's looking for troublemakers like you, Domingo. I'd learn to sleep with one eye open if I were you. *(MIER-COLES exits.)*

DOMINGO. La Llorona, which Miercoles sometimes called La Viuda Martinez, had been a story passed on in my family for generations. La Llorona is a story filled with tragedy and guilt. Most Mexican stories are. *(DOMINGO picks up a baseball.)* I loved playing baseball when I was a kid but I had no one to play with. All my sisters ever wanted to do was to play dolls, play house or play dress up. Worst of all they hated baseball! I had no one to play with.

(MIERCOLES and VIERNES enter with dolls.)

DOMINGO *(as a boy)*. Hey, Miercoles, Viernes, you guys wanna play some catch?

MIERCOLES. No.

VIERNES *(imitating MIERCOLES)*. No.

DOMINGO. Me against you two?!

MIERCOLES. No.

VIERNES. No.

DOMINGO. I'll let you win?! Please...?

MIERCOLES. Only if you play dolls with us?

VIERNES. Only if you play dolls with us?

DOMINGO. No way!

MIERCOLES. You can be Ken!

VIERNES. Yeah, you can be Ken!

DOMINGO. I don't think so.

MIERCOLES. Suit yourself, Worm.

VIERNES. Yeah, suit yourself...

DOMINGO & MIERCOLES. Be quiet!

VIERNES. What?!

MIERCOLES. You sound like an "echo"! Stop repeating everything I say!

VIERNES. Jeez, you two always pick on me! 'Amá! *(VIERNES exits.)*

MIERCOLES. Wait, Viernes, don't you want to play dolls? *(MIERCOLES exits.)*

DOMINGO. Sisters. All they're ever good for is making life horrible. I always got even with them though. You see, I'd switch their dolls around. Doll parts and everything. They'd get angry at one another thinking the other sister had done it. I never said a thing!

(A roar of a crowd is heard as DOMINGO plays baseball by himself. An ANNOUNCER's voice is heard calling the game.)

ANNOUNCER *(voice-over)*. It's the bottom of the ninth and the count is full at Chavez Ravine. What incredible pressure this young man must be feeling today. Sanchez steps up to the plate. But, wait, the young Dodger sensation is tipping his hat to the Giants' pitcher. Now, he's making faces. What could this mean? Sanchez digs in. *(The sound of a baseball pitch is heard hurtling toward DOMINGO. DOMINGO swings and hits it. The crowd roars.)* Oh, my gosh, it's back, back, way back!! Domingo Sanchez has hit a thundering home run out of Chavez Ravine! *(DOMINGO starts running the imaginary bases.)* He's rounding the bases. Waving to his family and friends. Stopping for a Dodger dog and a Coca-Cola. The Dodgers are the world champions! The world champions!

DOMINGO. Where'd my baseball go? Oh, no... I hit it over into the La Viuda Martinez' yard. The Black Widow Spider's house! Nothing ever comes back from there! I could see my ball just over the fence. It was right there among the weeds staring me right in the face. Calling to me. "Domingo, ayudame!" What should I do? We're not supposed to go into other people's yards. "Domingo, apurate!" So I decided to go after it. I jumped over La Viuda Martinez' fence. Then suddenly the house looked bigger than before. And the paint was cracking and the house creaked. It kinda looked like the Addam's Family house except there were no clouds or thunder. (*The crack of thunder is heard.*) Maybe there was thunder. The weeds suddenly were real tall. Her whole yard was like a jungle. (*The sound of jungle animals are heard.*) What was that?! Oh, it just kept getting worse. Lions, tigers and bears. Suddenly I heard a door open.

MARTINEZ. Ah huh, I finally found you, Perro Pestoso!

DOMINGO. "What should I do?! Where's the fence?!" I heard footsteps!

(*MARTINEZ enters holding a broom. They bump into each other scaring each other.*)

DOMINGO. Aghhh!!

MARTINEZ. Agghhh!!

DOMINGO & MARTINEZ. Agghhh!!

DOMINGO. I got so scared I fainted! (*DOMINGO faints.*)

MARTINEZ. Ay, Dios, mio! Que susto! (*She crosses to DOMINGO.*) Muchacho, are you all right?! Wake up!

DOMINGO (*awakening*). 'Amá? Do I have to go to school today?

MARTINEZ. Good, you're alive! No bones broken. I thought you were that stinky dog, Perro Pestoso. He's always leaving me little surprises.

DOMINGO. I awoke in a strange place. It didn't look like my house. I lay on a couch that wasn't mine. And there she was, La Viuda Martinez looking right into my eyes.

MARTINEZ. Muchacho, who gave you permission to come into my yard?!

DOMINGO. It wasn't my fault. Please don't turn me into a rock!

MARTINEZ. A rock? Que dices? *(She looks straight into his eyes, then exits.)*

DOMINGO. 'Amá!! I ran out of there as fast as I could. "I looked right into her eyes! I'm gonna turn into a rock! I don't want to be a rock!" *(Realizing.)* "I'm not a rock! It pays to be an altar boy!" I went home and told Miercoles who made fun of me and Viernes who ratted to mom. I got spanked for jumping in La Viuda Martinez' yard.

(DICIEMBRE enters and hands DOMINGO a plate covered in foil.)

DICIEMBRE. Toma, take these tamales to la Señora Martinez and tell her you're sorry for causing trouble.

DOMINGO. That's my mom, Diciembre. December. *(To DICIEMBRE.)* But, 'Amá I escaped from her house. De veras, she almost turned me into a rock.

DICIEMBRE. Que dices?

DOMINGO. Everyone on Calabasas Street thinks she's crazy, 'Amá. Some say she is a bruja. Miercoles says she's La Llorona.

DICIEMBRE. Don't believe everything you hear, Domingo. You make sure you apologize to Señora Martinez.

DOMINGO. But, 'Amá, she collects junk and brings it home. No one sees what she does with it. Isn't that loco?

DICIEMBRE. Mira, Le Señora Martinez es una viuda.

DOMINGO. I know she's a widow. Miercoles calls her the Black Widow Spider.

DICIEMBRE. I'll talk with your sister later. La Señora Martinez vive solita. Esa señora no es loca. No tiene marido que la cuide. Andale, levale estos tamales.

DOMINGO. Do I have to?

DICIEMBRE. Yes.

DOMINGO. But, 'Amá, if I go I'll never come back.

DICIEMBRE. Andale!

DOMINGO. You're sending me to her house never to be seen again. The police will arrest you if I don't come back.

DICIEMBRE. Andale! Miercoles! *(She exits.)*

DOMINGO. I prayed all the way to la Loca's house. "Please, Diosito, watch over me. And just in case I don't come back, make sure my sisters don't get any toys for Christmas." I knocked on the door real quiet so maybe she wouldn't hear me.

(A door is heard creaking open and MARTINEZ enters. DOMINGO turns his head away.)

MARTINEZ. Muchacho, you came back?

DOMINGO. I had to. My mom made me. She said I had to apologize to you for causing so much trouble. So, sorry! Okay! Bye!

MARTINEZ. Wait! Is there something wrong with your neck?

DOMINGO. No.

MARTINEZ. What smells so good?

DOMINGO. Tamales. They're for you. Can I go now?

MARTINEZ *(mysterious)*. No, I have something for you.

DOMINGO. You do?

MARTINEZ. Ven conmigo.

DOMINGO. But I really have to go.

MARTINEZ. Are you afraid?

DOMINGO. Ah, ... no ...

MARTINEZ. Good. This way.

DOMINGO. We went into her house. *(To himself.)* "Don't look at her eyes! She'll turn you into a rock."

MARTINEZ. It's around here somewhere. Where could it be?

DOMINGO. We walked through that old dark creaky house. She collected everything. It looked like a junk-yard.

MARTINEZ. Oh, I left it in the cuartito!

DOMINGO. "What room?" I asked. Certain my life was about to end. It felt like the ending of some tragic Mexican movie my mom liked to watch on Saturday afternoons. "What room?" I repeated.

MARTINEZ. Where I keep the children.

DOMINGO. Children?

MARTINEZ *(mysterious)*. You'll see.

DOMINGO. Oh, no, I looked into her eyes!

MARTINEZ. Follow me if you dare.

DOMINGO. She led me down a dark hallway. And there at the end of it stood a large door. The tiny little hairs on the back of neck stood up. She unlocked the door with a big key.

MARTINEZ. Have you been a good boy?

DOMINGO. Me?

MARTINEZ. Sí, tú.

DOMINGO. My mom calls me her little angel and she's expecting me back real soon. Did I mention my uncle is in the Mexican Mafia?

MARTINEZ. Wait here.

DOMINGO. She went into the room alone. "Okay, feet, let's go." Nothing. "What is she doing? Is this what happened to all the other children?" I was afraid and curious at the same time. Like a good scary movie. I had to look. So I opened the door slowly and what I saw will remain with me for the rest of my life.

(Music. Lights rise on all kinds of beautiful piñatas. They look more like sculptures.)

DOMINGO. Wow!

MARTINEZ. These are my children.

DOMINGO. They're piñatas!

MARTINEZ. They live here in my cuartito.

DOMINGO. La Viuda Martinez, "la Loca" of Calabasas Street was a piñata collector.

MARTINEZ. No, no, I made them.

DOMINGO. "La Loca" of Calabasas Street was a misunderstood piñata maker! That's why she collected junk, so she could make piñatas!

MARTINEZ. Esto son mis hijos.

DOMINGO. They're your children?

MARTINEZ. Yes. I created every one of them. I make them from things that people throw away.

DOMINGO. They're real, real, real... Can I have one?

MARTINEZ. Oh, no, I'll never give away my children. I love them too dearly.

DOMINGO. They're not like the store-bought ones.

MARTINEZ. They're better. These are special piñatas.

DOMINGO. They are?

MARTINEZ. Watch and listen. *(She spins the piñatas and they become illuminated. Music is heard.)*

DOMINGO. How did you do that?

MARTINEZ. That's a secret! Can you keep a secret? *(DOMINGO nods his head. She whispers into his ear.)*

DOMINGO. That star piñata one is my favorite.

MARTINEZ. It's the North Star. Sailors use it to guide them home.

DOMINGO. How do you know that?

MARTINEZ. My husband, Kiko, was a sailor. He used to be out at sea for months.

DOMINGO. There's a barco...

MARTINEZ. And La Ballena...

DOMINGO. La Sirena...

MARTINEZ. El Pez... Ah, and here's your baseball.

DOMINGO. You found it!

MARTINEZ. By accident I must confess. I was scaring a neighbor's dog away, Perro Pestoso, and I thought you were him. I'm sorry I scared you with my broom.

DOMINGO. I'm sorry I ran away...

MARTINEZ. That's all right, muchacho. I've come to expect it from the neighborhood children. They think I'm crazy.

DOMINGO. I don't think you are.

MARTINEZ. You don't?

DOMINGO. Not anymore.

MARTINEZ. Como te llamas?

DOMINGO. My name's Domingo.

MARTINEZ. And mine is Consuelo. Mucho gusto. You better go before your mother starts to worry.

DOMINGO. Can I come back sometime?

MARTINEZ. If you wish. I would like that. *(She hands DOMINGO his baseball. She spits.)*

DOMINGO. Yuck!

MARTINEZ. Oh, forgive me... I love smoking cigars. It's a bad habit. One I should break. I learned it from my Tia, the revolutionary. She rode with Pancho Villa!

DOMINGO. Who's Pancho Villa?

MARTINEZ. You don't know who General Francisco Villa was?

DOMINGO. I think he pitched for the Dodgers, no?

MARTINEZ. He was a hero to the Mexican people. They even made a movie of him. *Viva Villa!* Probecito, he dies in the end. How tragic. *(She exits.)*

DOMINGO. I went home that day thinking "la Loca" wasn't really loca after all. She was an artist. The first one I ever met. She'd spend her day searching for junk no one wanted and by night she would create these beautiful works of art. That night when I went to sleep I dreamt about the sea and that I was a sea captain and I was looking for whales who spoke Spanish. There was La Sirena—The Mermaid. She sounded a lot like Teresa Garcia who sat behind me in the Mrs. Aguirre's third grade class. She'd wave and sing songs in Spanish to me. The next morning I wanted to visit La Viuda

Martinez and her piñatas. *(The sound of an alarm clock is heard.)* But there was school.

(DICIEMBRE enters.)

DICIEMBRE. Levantanse, sleepy head!

DOMINGO. And my mom. 'Amá, I can't to go to school today.

DICIEMBRE. Porqué no?

DOMINGO. I...feel...sick!

DICIEMBRE. De veras?

DOMINGO. Yeah.

DICIEMBRE. That's strange, you don't have a fever. Let me see your tongue.

DOMINGO. Ah,...well...it's inside. It's kinda an achy, icky, scratchy feeling.

DICIEMBRE. Maybe I should call the doctor?

DOMINGO. Oh, I don't think it's that bad. Maybe I should just stay home today, huh?

DICIEMBRE. I heard there's this real bad flu from China and you get so sick that you can't eat anything.

DOMINGO. Is that why children are starving in China?

DICIEMBRE. No, mijo. Who told you that?

DOMINGO. You.

DICIEMBRE. I better get you some Vicks. And I'll call your nana to make you some menudo.

DOMINGO. Menudo?! *(To audience.)* I hate menudo! Cow guts! Yuck! *(To DICIEMBRE.)* 'Amá, I don't think I should eat menudo because I think it'll make me feel worse.

DICIEMBRE. You'll have to have lots of it. Menudo for breakfast, lunch and dinner. Ay, your father is going to

be so happy you're sick. He loves eating your grand-
mother's menudo. Well, I better call your nana.

DOMINGO *(aside)*. We should send Nana and her menudo
to China. *(To DICIEMBRE.)* 'Amá, I feel a lot better!
The achy, icky, scratchy feeling is gone! It's a miracle!
It's a miracle on Calabasas Street!

DICIEMBRE. De veras...?

DOMINGO. Yeah, I think I don't have the flu you're talking about. Maybe I ate something, or something...

DICIEMBRE. Mira, Domingo, I know you were pretending
and that won't get you too far with me. Te conosco, Mosco!

DOMINGO. Miercoles does it all the time!

DICIEMBRE. Miercoles, ven aca! Andale!

(MIERCOLES enters followed by VIERNES.)

MIERCOLES. What, 'Amá?

VIERNES. What, 'Amá?

DICIEMBRE. You're all in deep trouble. As punishment
everyone is eating menudo tonight! Sopas!

MIERCOLES & VIERNES. We hate menudo! *(DICIEM-
BRE exits.)*

DOMINGO. I wish I was in China!!

MIERCOLES. Thanks a lot, you worm!

VIERNES. Jeez!

*(DICIEMBRE enters carrying three large grocery-bag
sack lunches with their names written on them.)*

DICIEMBRE. Here's your sack lunches. Andale, next time
think about your little mentiritas. Mothers have radar for
that! Don't be late for school.

(DICIEMBRE exits. The school BUS DRIVER enters holding a steering wheel.)

BUS DRIVER. Okay, muchachitos, it's time for school! Get on board y vamonos! *(They follow the BUS DRIVER as he circles the stage.)*

MIERCOLES. You're gonna pay, Domingo! You're gonna wish you were never born.

VIERNES. Just thinking about menudo makes me sick! Nana makes big pots of menudo that last forever!

DOMINGO. I wasn't trying to get you in trouble. I wanted to visit La Señora Martinez, and I thought by pretending I was sick...

MIERCOLES. Are you crazy?!

DOMINGO. No!

MIERCOLES. The Black Widow Spider must have you under her spell.

DOMINGO. I was gonna bring her some limones is all.

MIERCOLES. That's how it starts. With fruit, Loco! Let me see your eyes.

DOMINGO. What is it?!

VIERNES. What is it?

MIERCOLES. Exactly as I thought! You got loco eyes!

VIERNES. 'Amá!!

DOMINGO & MIERCOLES. Shut up!

DOMINGO. You're telling lies, Miercoles. La Señora Martinez is a real nice person.

MIERCOLES. That's what all the other children said. And look what happened them?

VIERNES. What happened to them?!

MIERCOLES. They never returned home. Their mothers and fathers cry all night because she took them away and now they're probably worm food or worse, menudo.

DOMINGO. I don't believe you.

VIERNES. I believe you!

MIERCOLES. Listen, Domingo, since you won't be coming back, you think I could have your G.I. Joe? He'd make a great boyfriend for my Barbie?

DOMINGO. What are you talking about?

VIERNES. Yeah? What are you talking about?

MIERCOLES. Is there an echo? Let me spell it out for you. Nobody ever comes out of her house twice. She was probably being nice to you so she can lure you back in and do something terrible to you. So, since you won't be coming back I want your G.I. Joe for my Barbie, 'kay?

DOMINGO. You're sick!

VIERNES. Don't go to her house, Domingo!

DOMINGO. She's a nice lady, Viernes. There's nothing to be afraid of. Look what you've done, Miercoles, you've scared her.

MIERCOLES. I'd rather be scared than sorry.

BUS DRIVER. We're here! La escuela! *(The bus stops and the BUS DRIVER holds a small American flag. They stand at attention.)*

ALL. I pledge allegiance to the flag... *(They all freeze except for DOMINGO.)*

DOMINGO. School seemed like forever! Mrs. Aguirre was sick and we had a substitute teacher named Mr. Moyer.

ALL. Blah, blah, blah, blah, blah, blah...

DOMINGO. All he talked about was fishing trips.

ALL. Blah, blah, blah, blah, blah, blah...

DOMINGO. I couldn't wait to get home.

ALL. Blah, blah, blah, blah, blah, blah...

(A school bell is heard. VIERNES, MIERCOLES and the BUS DRIVER exit. DICIEMBRE is heard singing in Span-ish while she hands imaginary clothes out to dry. DOM-INGO begins picking imaginary lemons.)

DOMINGO. When I got home from school I picked some limones from our backyard lemon tree and I thought I'd take them to La Viuda Martinez. Is that all right, Mom?

DICIEMBRE. That's fine, pero; don't expect because your being nice that your not gonna eat menudo tonight.

DOMINGO. No, 'Amá...

DICIEMBRE. Your Nana made a big pot of it! You'll eat everything she serves. *(DICIEMBRE exits singing.)*

DOMINGO. You know, I think menudo was invented to torture little Mexican kids. My mother loved singing to her pet parrot, Chulo. He was green, feathery and foul mouthed. My father taught him all the bad words. Any-way, Chulo got old and died one day, so my mother put him in the freezer among the frozen meat, vegetables and ice cream. She had this idea that if she kept Chulo in the freezer he would become freeze-dried. Then she could take him out and put him on a shelf like a statue or something. Kinda like Roy Rogers did to his horse, Trigger. Well, it never did work out so she kept him in the freezer. I hated getting things out of the freezer be-cause Chulo was always there staring at you. One day, Miercoles speared Chulo with a stick. Like a popsicle, Imagine that, Chulo on a stick? When I got to La Viuda Martinez' house it seemed abandoned, as if she had her

own personal desert. It looked like a real sad house. I
knocked on her door.

(MARTINEZ enters.)

MARTINEZ. Go away?! I don't read the *Watch Tower!*

DOMINGO. It's me, Domingo. I brought you some limones!

MARTINEZ. Domingo?! I thought you were the Hallelu-
jahs. They're always trying to save me. *(Suddenly.)* Ay,
Dios mio! Come, quickly!

DOMINGO. What is it?!

MARTINEZ. I need your help! *(Classical music is heard.)*

DOMINGO. We rushed down the hall and into the cuartito
where she had all her piñatas. I found a little workshop
of piñatas. An assembly line of beginnings, half done
and finished piñatas.

MARTINEZ. Start cutting newspaper! Lots of it!

DOMINGO *(he does).* There! I'm finished!

MARTINEZ. Mix more glue, flour and water. Hurry!

DOMINGO. Done!

MARTINEZ. Muy bien!

DOMINGO. For the next hour La Viuda Martinez shaped
and formed a new piñata and I helped! Watching her
hands move so quickly here and there she looked like a
musical conductor leading an orchestra on some musical
journey.

MARTINEZ. There! It's finished!

DOMINGO. It's your house.

MARTINEZ. Yes!

DOMINGO. I've never seen it look that way before. All
the weeds are gone.

MARTINEZ. It used to be like that once long ago.

DOMINGO. Who are the two people standing in front?

MARTINEZ. My husband, Kiko, and I.

DOMINGO. What happened to your husband?

MARTINEZ. He died at sea.

(A special rises on KIKO. He is a memory.)

MARTINEZ. Kiko was a fisherman.

KIKO. I've planted rosas, nopales and all kinds of flowers for you.

MARTINEZ. You spoil me.

KIKO. You have the most beautiful yard in the neighborhood. Promise me you'll take care of it while I'm gone?

MARTINEZ. I don't know anything about plants.

KIKO. It's simple. All you have to do is water and talk to the plantitas. They grow with love, Amor.

MARTINEZ. People might think I'm crazy if I talk to plants.

KIKO. Let them. Promise me.

MARTINEZ. I promise. *(KIKO exits.)* He never came back. Looking at the yard reminded me so much of him that I let it go. I never kept my promise. You better go. *(She exits.)*

DOMINGO. I felt sad for Señora Martinez and for the future she never got with her husband. As I walked home I could see our neighbor's houses decorated with a whole lot of love and pride. Their yards so well kept. I thought about Señora Martinez and how sometimes the things people say about somebody aren't always true. She wasn't really crazy. Just a little misunderstood and lonely. Then it hit me. "Señora Martinez needs a friend! And I know just how to help!"

(DICIEMBRE enters singing.)

DOMINGO. 'Amá! 'Amá?!

DICIEMBRE. What is it, mijito?

DOMINGO. 'Amá, is it possible to use Papá's gardening tools?

DICIEMBRE. Pero porqué los quieres?

DOMINGO. I'm gonna fix up la Señora Martinez' yard!

DICIEMBRE. Como que "fix up"?

DOMINGO. Yeah, I'm gonna make her yard green again like it once was. Just like in the piñata!

(MIERCOLES and VIERNES enter.)

MIERCOLES. Is Domingo in trouble?!

VIERNES. Is Domingo in trouble?!

MIERCOLES. Stop it!

VIERNES. What?!

DOMINGO. 'Amá, Señora Martinez makes piñatas. Her Tia Pancho Villa taught her.

MIERCOLES. Pancho Villa?

VIERNES. Pancho Villa?

DICIEMBRE. Why are you doing this, mijo? Don't expect that you'll get extra presents this Christmas.

MIERCOLES *(to VIERNES)*. That's why he's doing it.

DOMINGO. No, 'Amá. It's a promise I gotta help her keep.

DICIEMBRE. Bueno pues, go ask your father. I don't think he'll mind. I'm proud of you, mijo. Sometimes you surprise me. You can be an angel.

DOMINGO. Thanks! You wanna help, Viernes?

VIERNES. Okay. *(DOMINGO, DICIEMBRE and VIER-NES exit.)*

MIERCOLES. So he's gonna help out "la loca," huh? He's crazy as she is. Loony birds! I've seen this sick psycho stuff before. Your gonna pay, Domingo. Mom always thinks you're the angel of the family. Well, I got news for you. You won't be the angel for long cause I'm the angel wing-clipper. Oh, Viernes...

(MIERCOLES exits. DOMINGO enters.)

DOMINGO. That Saturday I began working on La Viuda Martinez' yard. I wanted to surprise her. I cleaned all the dry brush and weeds away. It was hard work. But it was fun too. I found this super-dooper diamond. See?! I know it looks like a piece of glass, but it's not! *(He pulls out a large piece of glass.)* It's gotta be real. Look at the size of it! I'm gonna save it for my mom's birthday. She'll be real surprised. She's never had a diamond ring before! *(He puts the glass away.)* By the afternoon, I had planted fresh flowers that I brought from home. Señora Martinez' yard sorta looked like ours. I even added some of our statues like Bambi, Cantinflas and Vicky Carr. It looked real good!

(MIERCOLES and VIERNES enter.)

MIERCOLES. What are you doing, Domingo?

VIERNES. Yeah, what are you doing, Domingo?

MIERCOLES. Stop it.

VIERNES. Jeez!

DOMINGO. What do you want, Miercoles?

MIERCOLES. Nothing. I just wanted to tell you how proud I am of you.

DOMINGO. Huh?

MIERCOLES. Well, you fixed La Crazy... I mean, Señora Martinez' yard real nice.

VIERNES. Real nice.

MIERCOLES. And I think you're a real super bro.

VIERNES. Super.

DOMINGO. For reals?

MIERCOLES (*crossing her fingers behind her back*). For reals. Cross my heart.

DOMINGO. Thanks.

MIERCOLES. Is she around?

DOMINGO. No, she's out looking for stuff.

MIERCOLES. Do you think we could look at the piñatas?

DOMINGO. Well...

MIERCOLES. Maybe there aren't any piñatas. Huh, Viernes?

VIERNES. Guess not.

DOMINGO. Sure there are!

MIERCOLES. Then why don't you show us?

DOMINGO. Because I'm the only person that can go inside her house. She told me.

MIERCOLES. Well, I don't see her anywhere. And what she don't see, she don't know, que no?

DOMINGO. I don't think it's a good idea.

MIERCOLES. There aren't any piñatas in there. What a mentiroso!

DOMINGO. They do exist!

MIERCOLES. I dare you to show us!

DOMINGO. Fine! I'll prove you wrong! Come with me but you do as I say. (*To audience.*) We entered her house. I know we shouldn't have but we did. *(To MIER-COLES and VIERNES.)* Okay, we're in. Promise you won't touch a thing?

MIERCOLES & VIERNES. We promise.

(Lights rise on the piñatas.)

DOMINGO. There! I told you.

VIERNES. Wow!

MIERCOLES. They really are piñatas?

DOMINGO. That's what I've been telling you. This one's her favorite. *(He picks up the house piñata.)*

VIERNES. Can I touch it, Domingo?

DOMINGO. I guess if you're careful.

VIERNES. I'll be careful. *(VIERNES takes the piñata. MIER-COLES crosses to her and beings playing roughly with it.)*

MIERCOLES. Let me see!

DOMINGO. What are you doing?!

MIERCOLES. Just playing with it. We have to be careful, Viernes. We don't want to break it. There might be evil spirits inside.

VIERNES. Huh?

MIERCOLES. We wouldn't want them to come and get you. Give it to me!

VIERNES. Domingo!

DOMINGO. Stop it, Miercoles! *(DOMINGO crosses to MIERCOLES. He attempts to take it away from her.)*

MIERCOLES. Maybe it's got candy inside!

DOMINGO. Let go, Miercoles! *(MIERCOLES and DOM-INGO tear the piñata in half.)* Oh, no, it's broken!

MIERCOLES. It wasn't my fault, Domingo. You wouldn't let go! You're always the angel in the family!

MARTINEZ (*offstage*). I'm back!

MIERCOLES. What are we gonna do?!

DOMINGO. We got to fix it!

(*MARTINEZ enters.*)

MARTINEZ. What are you doing here? What happened to
my piñata?

DOMINGO. It's my fault, Señora Martinez...

MARTINEZ. You did this?

DOMINGO. It was an accident.

MARTINEZ. You ruined it! (*MARTINEZ begins to cry.*)

MIERCOLES. She's crying, Domingo.

VIERNES (*starting to cry*). I want my 'amá.

MARTINEZ. Get out of my house! Get out!

DOMINGO. Señora Martinez, can you ever forgive me?

(*KIKO appears. Everyone freezes except for MARTINEZ.*)

KIKO. Consuelo, come and look at the yard.

MARTINEZ. Kiko...?

KIKO. Isn't it beautiful?

MARTINEZ. There're so many flowers. There's statues of
Bambi, Cantinflas and Vicki Carr. Who did all this?

KIKO. The boy.

MARTINEZ. Domingo?

KIKO. You kept your promise. (*KIKO holds out a rose to
her. Lights fade on him.*)

DOMINGO. Señora Martinez, can you ever forgive me?

MIERCOLES. It's all my fault.

MARTINEZ. It's all right. Aren't piñatas made to be broken?

DOMINGO (*to audience*). Huh?

MARTINEZ. They're only piñatas! I want you each to pick one and take it home with you!

DOMINGO. But they're your children.

MARTINEZ. I'd rather have friends. Besides, we can always make more. I'll show you how.

DOMINGO, MIERCOLES & VIERNES. Gracias, Señora Martinez. (MIERCOLES and VIERNES exit.)

MARTINEZ. Domingo?

DOMINGO. Yes, Señora?

MARTINEZ. Thank you for being my friend. (She exits.)

(DICIEMBRE, MIERCOLES and VIERNES enter.)

DICIEMBRE. What beautiful piñatas!

DOMINGO. They're from Señora Martinez.

MIERCOLES. Can we invite her over to dinner sometime?

DICIEMBRE. Que milagro?

DOMINGO. I think she'd come, 'Amá.

DICIEMBRE. Bueno pues, I better start planning Thanksgiving. I'll call your nana to make us some menudo!

MIERCOLES. Menudo?!

DOMINGO. Menudo?!

VIERNES. Do I hear an echo?

DICIEMBRE (exiting). I know! Tacos with menudo! Tamales with menudo! Or menudo with chile con carne! (VIERNES and MIERCOLES follow her out.)

DOMINGO. La Viuda Martinez did accept our dinner offer and many more after that. She taught us how to make piñatas and look at the world in a whole new way! Miercoles, my troublemaker sister, the pain of my existence, became a dentist. Viernes, the tattletale, became a cable talk-show host. My mom got another parrot. And I took care of La Viuda Martinez' yard until I went away to college. I'll never forget her and the gift she gave to me.

(Lights rise on MARTINEZ. She spits loudly.)

DOMINGO. Ah, that's sweet!

MUSIC—END OF PLAY

CALABASAS STREET
Glossary

Pg. #

8   **Mira, es la loca!** - Look, it's the crazy one!
bruja - witch
viuda - widow
Tio/Tia - Uncle/Aunt

9   **Mocosco** - snot-nose

12   **"Domingo, ayudame!"** - Domingo, help me!
"Domingo, apurate!" - Domingo, hurry up!
Ay, Dios, mio! Que susto. - Oh, God, what a fright.

13   **Que dices** - What did you say?

14   **Mira, La Señora Martinez es una viuda.** - Look, Señora
Martinez is a widow

**La Señora Martinez vive solita. Esa señora no es loca.
No tiene marido que la cuide. Andale, levale estos tamales.**
Señora Martinez lives alone. That woman isn't crazy. She has
no husband to care for her. Go on, take these tamales to her.

Andale! Miercoles! - Come on! Miercoles!

15   **Ven conmigo.** - Come with me.
cuartito - little room

16   **Esto son mis hijos.** - These are my children.

17   **barco** - a boat
La Ballena - a whale

17   **El Pez** - a fish

18   **Como te llamas?** - What's your name?
     Mucho gusto. - With pleasure.
     Probecito - Poor little one

19   **La sirena, a mermaid**
     Levantanse, sleepy heads! - Wake up, sleepy heads!
     Porqué no? - Why not?
     De veras? - Really?
     No, mijo. - No, son.
     menudo - tripe

20   **De veras...?** - Really...?
     Te conosco, Mosco! - I know you, Mosco!
     ven aca! Andale! - come here. Now!
     Sopas! - An expression: "There you go!"
     mentiritas - little lies

21   **y vamonos!** - and let's go!

22   **La escuela!** - The school!

25   **nopales** - cactus

26   **mijito** - son
     Pero porqué los quieres? - Why do you want them?
     Como que "fix up"? - What do you mean "fix up"?
     Bueno pues, Well,

28   **mentiroso!** - liar!

31   **Que milagro?** - What a miracle?

DIRECTOR'S NOTES

DIRECTOR'S NOTES

DIRECTOR'S NOTES

DIRECTOR'S NOTES

DIRECTOR'S NOTES

DIRECTOR'S NOTES